Fact Finders®

WORLD EXPLORERS

HENRY HUDSON

An Explorer of the Northwest Passage

by Amie Hazleton

CAPSTONE PRESS
a capstone imprint

Fact Finders Books are published by Capstone Press,
1710 Roe Crest Drive, North Mankato, Minnesota 56003
www.mycapstone.com

Library of Congress Cataloging-in-Publication Data
Names: Hazelton, Amie, author.
Title: Henry Hudson : an explorer of the Northwest Passage / by Amie Hazelton.
Description: North Mankato, Minnesota : Capstone Press, 2017. | Series: Fact
  finders. World explorers | Includes bibliographical references and index. |
  Audience: Grades 4–6.
Identifiers: LCCN 2016025966 | ISBN 9781515742050 (library binding) | ISBN
  9781515742098 (pbk.) | ISBN 9781515742517 (eBook PDF)
Subjects: LCSH: Hudson, Henry, –1611—Juvenile literature. | Explorers—America—
  Biography—Juvenile literature. | Explorers—Great Britain—Biography—Juvenile
  literature. | America—Discovery and exploration—British—Juvenile literature. |
  Hudson River Valley (N.Y. and N.J.)—Discovery and exploration—Juvenile
  literature.Classification: LCC E129.H8 H29 2017 | DDC 910.92 [B]—dc23
LC record available at https://lccn.loc.gov/2016025966

Editorial Credits:
Alesha Sullivan, editor; Kayla Rossow, designer; Wanda Winch, media researcher;
Laura Manthe, production specialist

Photo Credits:
Bridgeman Images: ©Look and Learn/Private Collection/Peter Jackson, 27, ©Look
and Learn/Private Collection/Severino Baraldi, 13, Pictures From History, 23;
Capstone, 5; Getty Images: The LIFE Picture Collection/Mansell, 16; Granger,
NYC - All rights reserved/Sarin Images, 8; iStockphoto: leezsnow, cover inset;
North Wind Picture Archives, 6, 15, 18, 19, 24; Shutterstock: Ana de Sousa, 11, arigato,
cardboard texture, Ensuper, scratch paper texture, Everett Historical, 7, gans33, 12,
Kris Grabiec, cover background, Melinda Fawver, 21, Nik Merkulov, grunge paper
element, run4it, watercolor paper element, Sunny Forest, sky design element

Printed in China.
009943S17

TABLE OF CONTENTS

Introduction

The Passage to Asia

In 1607 Henry Hudson began making preparations for the first of his four famous trips of exploration. Hudson was an expert **navigator** and a skilled sailor. He had been hired by the Muscovy Company in England to locate a quick route to Asia. China and Japan possessed luxury goods, such as spices, silks, jewels, and gold.

Between 1607 and 1611, Hudson made four **voyages** in search of a passage to Asia. Hudson's **expeditions** and successes are well known. Although he never found a shorter route from Europe to Asia, his trips were important.

navigator—a person who directs the route of a ship, aircraft, or other form of transportation, especially by using maps and instruments

voyage—a long journey

expedition—a long journey for a special purpose, such as exploring

Hudson's expeditions added to Europe's knowledge of the rest of the world. Hudson explored the coasts of Iceland, Greenland, and other islands in the Arctic Ocean. During his third journey, he became the first European to explore the Hudson River region. Hudson claimed the area for the Netherlands, calling it New Netherlands. Soon after, Dutch settlements in New Netherlands sprang up in what are now Connecticut, Delaware, New Jersey, and New York.

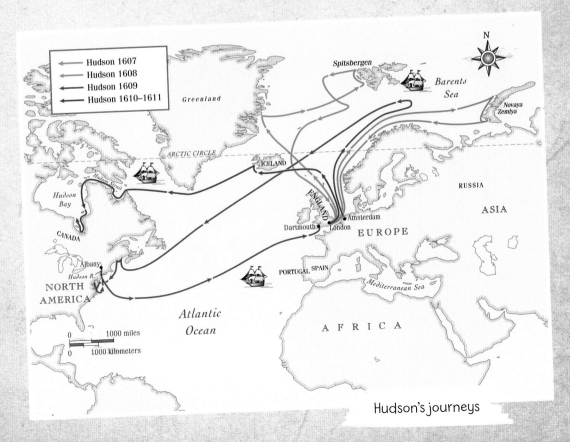

Hudson's journeys

Some mysteries still surround the explorer. Where did Hudson come from? How did he gain his knowledge and experience of sailing? Very little is known of Hudson before 1607. He may have been born around 1565, but it is not certain. There are no written records of his birth, childhood, or early adult life. Some **historians** think that Hudson may have been the grandson of a London public official. Others believe Hudson's family was somehow connected to the Muscovy Company.

Henry Hudson

Hudson met American Indians at Sandy Hook, New York, in 1609.

In 1497 the Portuguese had established the first sea route from Europe to Asia, with the help of explorer Vasco de Gama. They made the trip by sailing around the southern tip of Africa. The Portuguese route was difficult, exhausting, and expensive. Many European explorers had talked about finding a better route to Asia. The rush was on to be the first explorer to find such a route.

Chapter 1

ADVENTURES ON THE HOPEWELL

The Muscovy Company was eager to be the first to find a northern route to Asia. The Dutch had controlled trade with Asia since the early 1600s. As a result the British company had fallen on hard times and was not making much money. The company needed to be successful at locating a faster route to Asia if it wanted to stay in business.

In Hudson's day, many Europeans believed that Asia could be reached by sailing straight across the North Pole.

In 1607 the Muscovy Company hired Hudson. They gave him command of a ship called the *Hopewell*. On April 23, Hudson and his crew of 11 men set sail from London. Hudson left behind his wife, Katherine, and his sons Oliver and Richard. He brought along his young son, John, who worked as Hudson's assistant.

By the beginning of May, the *Hopewell* had lost sight of the English coast. For six weeks, Hudson and his crew sailed northwest through the Atlantic Ocean. On June 15 they came upon the western shore of Greenland. They continued along Greenland's northward coast, slowly making their way through fog and floating ice.

By the end of June, Hudson came upon Spitsbergen Island, just east of Greenland. From there the crew headed north, hoping to make their way across the North Pole. Members of the group spotted many whales, seals, and walruses. As Hudson continued to sail north, he began to suspect the worst. By July they were still about 575 miles (925 kilometers) away from the North Pole. Hudson realized the *Hopewell* would never make it past the North Pole. The water was thick with ice. Hudson turned around and headed back to London.

The *Hopewell* reached London in September. Hudson had not succeeded in finding a quicker route to Asia. But the Muscovy Company still considered his voyage a success. They soon began sending whaling ships to Spitsbergen to hunt whales for their blubber. The blubber would then be boiled down into oil, which fueled lamps and candles. This was the beginning of the English whaling **industry**.

The following year the Muscovy Company paid for Hudson to make a second voyage. This time the explorer would sail along the northern coast of Russia looking for a route to Asia. This **rumored** route was called the Northeast Passage.

Once again Hudson commanded the *Hopewell.* Hudson's son, John, joined him again for the second voyage, along with 13 others. On April 22, 1608, the *Hopewell* once again sailed out of London's harbor. It sailed northeast, rounding the tip of Norway in late May. The awful cold weather and fog made some of the crew very sick.

industry—a business that produces a product or provides a service
rumor—something said by many people although it may not be true

The *Hopewell* needed to be able to sail through icy waters. Its hull, or body, was strengthened for Hudson's second voyage.

Ice was the biggest threat to the *Hopewell* and its crew. In June the ship was nearly stuck in the ice off the coast of Norway. At other times the crew kept the ship away from danger by pushing the ice away with oars and poles.

By the end of June, the *Hopewell* reached the western coast of two islands called Novaya Zemlya. These islands were located to the north of Russia. There, some of the crew landed and searched for food and water. They returned with reports of seeing deer, bear, and fox tracks.

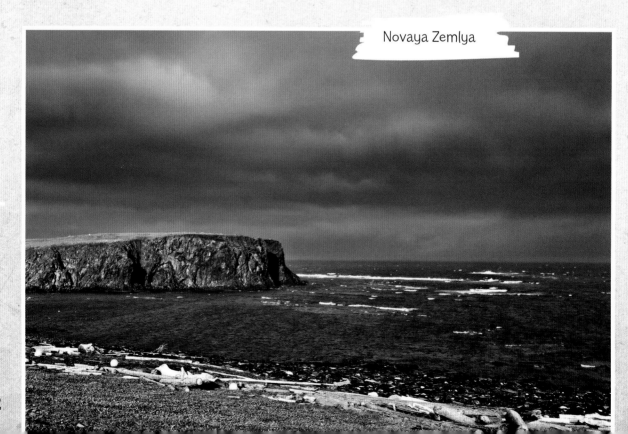

Novaya Zemlya

For more than a week, Hudson searched for a route around or through the islands. He tried to sail around Novaya Zemlya's northern tip, but ice blocked the way. Then Hudson spotted what looked like the mouth of a large river. He sent a few men to investigate. They soon brought back word that the river was too shallow for the *Hopewell*. Finally Hudson decided that he would not be able to find a way around Novaya Zemlya. The ship and its crew headed back to England.

an illustration of a mermaid seen by Hudson's crew

THE MYTH OF MERMAIDS

On June 15 two men reported seeing strange creatures in the waters. Hudson described them as having the body of a woman and the tail of a porpoise. On later voyages, other sailors reported seeing similar beasts. These mythical figures came to be called mermaids.

Chapter 2
A HISTORIC VOYAGE BEGINS

Hudson's first two voyages had been unsuccessful in finding a route to Asia. But Hudson was still confident such a route existed. The Muscovy Company, however, had lost faith in him. The company wouldn't pay for a third voyage. The company decided instead to spend its money on sending more whaling ships to Greenland.

Hudson was not ready to give up. He turned to the Netherlands and the Dutch East India Company to help pay for his next trip. This company already controlled European trade with Asia. And company officials were still interested in finding a quicker, shorter route to Asia.

The Dutch decided to give Hudson a chance. The explorer had more firsthand knowledge of the Arctic Ocean than anyone else. The company believed Hudson would succeed in finding the Northeast Passage.

In January 1609 Hudson signed a **contract** with the Dutch East India Company that required him to "search for a northeast passage, sailing north around Novaya Zemlya until he shall be able to sail south." The contract also required Hudson to turn over all his journals, **logs**, and charts at the end of the voyage. Just before Hudson set sail, the company added one last requirement: Hudson was not to look for any route but the Northeast Passage.

Dutch East India Company
in Amsterdam, Netherlands

contract—a legal agreement to do something
log—a written record

FACT!

In 1909 the Netherlands presented the United States with a replica of the *Half Moon* memorializing the 300th anniversary of Hudson's voyage.

The Dutch East India Company gave Hudson a small ship called the *Half Moon*. This little, flat-bottomed ship was about 60 feet (18 meters) long. It had two high decks on each end. Some of the crew were Dutch, and some were English. Hudson had problems with some of the crew to begin with because he did not speak Dutch.

In early April, the *Half Moon* set sail. Hudson led the ship up the coast of Norway. On May 5 the ship rounded Norway's North Cape and began heading east. The crew faced freezing temperatures, icy waters, and thick fog. The ship's sails froze in the freezing wind. Its ropes were coated with ice. The Dutch sailors were afraid. They were used to sailing the tropical waters of southern Asia. As their fear heightened, fighting broke out between the Dutch and English crewmembers.

By the middle of May, Hudson's crew was nearing **mutiny**. So Hudson went to his cabin and returned with letters and maps his friend Captain John Smith had sent him. Smith had explored the North American coast near Virginia. He had written to Hudson about a large mouth of water there. Perhaps this was the **Northwest Passage**, a supposed route through North America to Asia.

Hudson's ship, the *Half Moon*, leaving Amsterdam for the New World in 1609

mutiny—a revolt against the captain of a ship

Northwest Passage—a water route once believed to exist across North America, connecting the Atlantic and Pacific Oceans

CAPTAIN JOHN SMITH

Captain John Smith and Henry Hudson were great friends. Both men were from England and were skilled sailors. In 1607 Smith founded an English **colony** called Jamestown in Virginia. Jamestown was named for England's King James I. The colony became the first permanent English settlement in North America. He wrote to Hudson, describing the area's rivers and landscape. Smith described a possible waterway running across North America to the Pacific, leading Hudson to believe it was the Northwest Passage.

Using Captain John Smith's letters and maps as a guide, Hudson suggested the *Half Moon* search for the Northwest Passage instead of the Northeast Passage. The crew quickly agreed. Hudson turned the boat around, even though his contract with the Dutch said he could not do so. By May 19 the *Half Moon* was headed for North America.

colony—a territory settled by people from another country and controlled by that country

Chapter 3

EXPLORING THE HUDSON RIVER

On July 12, Hudson spotted North America. The ship anchored off the coast of Maine, and Hudson sent his men ashore to cut down trees for a new mast for the ship. The old one had been damaged during a violent storm.

From Maine Hudson continued down the coast. He sailed as far south as Cape Hatteras in what is present-day North Carolina. Then Hudson turned the boat around and headed back north. The captain followed the coastline until he reached present-day New Jersey. On September 3 Hudson sailed into what is known today as New York Bay.

Hudson and his crew spent the next few days exploring the region. On September 10 Hudson entered the river that would one day be named for him. The river was beautiful and full of fish. Hudson called it the "River of Mountains." The native people of the region called the river *Muhheakunnuk,* meaning "great waters constantly in motion."

The *Half Moon* sailed 150 miles (241 km) up the river. Along the way Hudson and his men traded with natives they met. The Europeans traded knives, beads, and hatchets in exchange

coast of Maine

for beaver and otter skins. At a point in the river just north of present-day Albany, New York, Hudson realized the river was too shallow to be the Northwest Passage. The *Half Moon* began its journey back down the river. Before Hudson left the area, he claimed the entire region for the Netherlands.

On October 4 the *Half Moon* left North America and headed back home. On November 7, Hudson docked in Dartmouth, England. He wrote a letter to the Dutch East India Company about his discoveries. The company wrote back and ordered Hudson to return to the Netherlands. English officials were angry with Hudson and held him on **house arrest**. Hudson had been exploring for a rival nation, and now officials demanded that he must only serve England.

In July 1610 the Dutch crew was released and headed back to the Netherlands with the *Half Moon*. The crew took all of Hudson's logs and maps with them. Unfortunately, these important records later disappeared.

house arrest—confinement by guards to one's home instead of a prison

All of Hudson's logs and journals belonged to the Dutch East India Company in Amsterdam.

Chapter 4

THE FINAL JOURNEY

Shortly after Hudson's third voyage, a group of wealthy English merchants wanted to send Hudson on a fourth trip. They hoped this time that he would be able to find the Northwest Passage. The merchants provided a ship called the *Discovery* for Hudson to use. The *Discovery* was an old ship, about 65 feet (20 m) long. The crew consisted of 20 men and two boys, including Hudson's son, John. The ship was filled with enough supplies to last eight months.

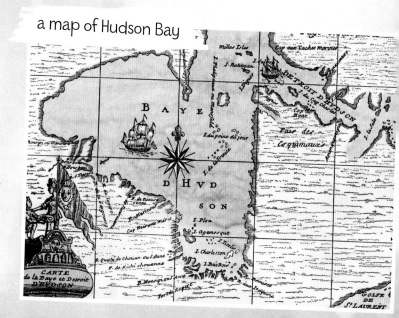

a map of Hudson Bay

On April 17, 1610, the *Discovery* left England and sailed north toward Iceland. By June 25 the crew had passed Greenland and entered a long strip of water that connects the Atlantic Ocean to what is now the Hudson Bay in Canada. It took the *Discovery* more than a month to travel through the rough and icy waters of the Hudson Bay. During this time the attitude of the crewmembers took a turn for the worse.

By the end of October, Hudson realized that he and his crew would be stuck in the bay for the winter. Hudson and his men were the first Europeans to spend the winter in the Arctic region.

The crew hauled the ship ashore and settled in for the cold months. Many crewmembers became sick because of the freezing temperatures and lack of food.

The crew was trapped in the Hudson Bay until June 1611. As the *Discovery* began to sail home, Hudson divided up what was left of the food among the men. Some of the men suspected Hudson hid extra food for himself. Led by Henry Greene and Robert Juet, the crew began plotting mutiny.

In mid-June the angry crewmembers attacked Hudson. They forced Hudson, his son, and seven other men onto a tiny boat. They had no food and no supplies. The crew aboard the *Discovery* cut the rope that was tied to the small boat. Then the *Discovery* sailed away. This was the last that is known of Hudson. In October the *Discovery* arrived back in London. The remaining crewmembers were never punished for their crime.

What happened to Henry Hudson remains a mystery. During his four voyages Hudson sailed to places never explored before. He proved that it was impossible to reach Asia by sailing across the North Pole. He made it possible for the Dutch to begin settling in the New York region. Today Henry Hudson's name lives on. Hudson Bay and Hudson Strait in Canada, and the Hudson River in New York, are all named to honor the brave explorer.

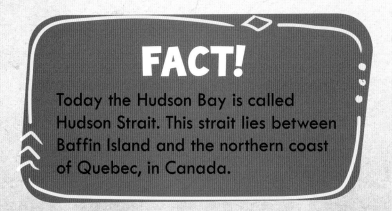

FACT!

Today the Hudson Bay is called Hudson Strait. This strait lies between Baffin Island and the northern coast of Quebec, in Canada.

An illustration shows Hudson was kicked off the *Discovery* and left to die.

Timeline

c. 1565: Henry Hudson is born in England

1607: Hudson goes on his first voyage and explores Greenland and the North Pole as captain of the *Hopewell*

1608: Hudson begins his second voyage on the *Hopewell*, this time traveling along the Russian coast in search of a passage to Asia

1609: The Dutch East India Company provides Hudson with the *Half Moon* to seek out the Northeast Passage; Hudson sails the Atlantic waters along the eastern North American coast and is able to claim the area of present-day New York for the Netherlands

1610-1611: Hudson commands the *Discovery* in an attempt to find the Northwest Passage; when he reaches the Arctic Ocean, his crew mutinies and sends Hudson adrift, never to be seen or heard from again

1614: At Katherine Hudson's request, the English East India Company heads an unsuccessful search to find Hudson

Important People

Henry Greene (?–1611)—formerly a friend of Hudson's, he helped lead the mutiny against Hudson and became captain after the explorer was set adrift

John Hudson (?–1611)—Henry's son, who was a victim of the 1611 mutiny; sailed with his father on several voyages

Robert Juet (?–1611)—member of Hudson's crew, who was a leader in the 1611 mutiny

John Smith (1580–1631)—friend of Hudson's and an explorer who settled the Jamestown colony of Virginia

GLOSSARY

colony (KOL-uh-nee)—a territory settled by people from another country and controlled by that country

contract (KAHN-trakt)—a legal agreement to do something

expedition (ek-spuh-DISH-uhn)—a long journey for a special purpose, such as exploring

historian (hi-STAWR-ee-uhn)—a person who studies past events

house arrest (HOUSS uh-REST)—confinement by guards to one's home instead of a prison

industry (IN-duh-stree)—a business which produces a product or provides a service

log (LOG)—a written record

mutiny (MYOOT-uh-nee)—a revolt against the captain of a ship

navigator (NAV-uh-gate-uhr)—a person who directs the route of a ship, aircraft, or other form of transportation, especially by using maps and instruments

Northwest Passage (NORTH-west PAS-ij)—a water route once believed to exist across North America connecting the Atlantic and Pacific Oceans

rumor (ROO-mur)—something said by many people although it may not be true

voyage (VOI-ij)—a long journey

READ MORE

Cooke, Tim. *Explore with Henry Hudson.* Travel with the Great Explorers. New York: Crabtree Publishing, 2014.

Waxman, Laura Hamilton. *A Journey with Henry Hudson.* Primary Source Explorers. Minneapolis, Minn.: Lerner Publications, 2016.

Sherman, Josepha, and Jack Connelly. *Henry Hudson: Exploring the Northwest Passage.* Incredible Explorers. New York: Cavendish Square Publishing, 2015.

INTERNET SITES

FactHound offers a safe, fun way to find Internet sites related to this book. All of the sites on FactHound have been researched by our staff.

Here's all you do:

Visit *www.facthound.com*

Type in this code: 9781515742050

Check out projects, games and lots more at
www.capstonekids.com

CRITICAL THINKING USING THE COMMON CORE

1. Why were the English and the Dutch so eager to find a short way to reach Asia? (Key Ideas and Details)

2. Why was Hudson arrested after he returned to England following his third voyage? (Key Ideas and Details)

3. Do you think Hudson's voyages were a success or failure? Why? (Integration of Knowledge and Ideas)

INDEX